IN RECITAL
Throughout the Year
(with Performance Strategies)

Volume One

ABOUT THE SERIES • A NOTE TO THE TEACHER

In Recital — Throughout the Year is a series that focuses on fabulous repertoire, intended to motivate your students. We know that to motivate, the teacher must challenge the student with attainable goals. This series makes that possible. The fine composers and arrangers of this series have created musically engaging pieces, which have been carefully leveled and address the technical strengths and weaknesses of students. The wide range of styles in each book of the series complements other FJH publications and will help you to plan students' recital repertoire for the entire year. You will find original solos and duets that focus on different musical and technical issues, giving you the selection needed to accommodate your students' needs. There are arrangements of famous classical themes, as well as repertoire written for Halloween, Christmas, and Fourth of July recitals. In this way, your student will have recital pieces throughout the entire year! Additionally, the series provides a progressive discussion on the art of performance. The earlier levels offer tips on recital preparation, while the later levels address more advanced technical and psychological issues that help to realize successful performances.

 Use the enclosed CD as a teaching and motivational tool. Have your students listen to the recording and discuss interpretation with you!

Production: Frank and Gail Hackinson
Production Coordinators: Philip Groeber and Isabel Otero Bowen
Cover: Terpstra Design, San Francisco
Text Design and Layout: Maritza Cosano Gomez
Engraving: Kevin R. Olson and Tempo Music Press, Inc.
Printer: Tempo Music Press, Inc.

ISBN 1-56939-392-3

9 Recital Preparation Tips • For the Teacher

1. Consider a tiered approach to developing comfort in performance. Make "mini" performances a regular occurrence, probably without even calling them performances. Have a student play for the student who follows his/her lesson. It doesn't matter if their leveling is different; the older students are naturally nice to the young and the young provide a non-threatening audience for the older. Have students play mini concerts at home. Younger students may enjoy concerts for their favorite stuffed animals each day after practice. Advise older students to practice performing by recording themselves. Of course, you will tailor these suggestions according to each student's personality. Just remember, *no venue is too small and frequency is the key*. Suggestions for mini-performances and performance strategies are also addressed in "A Note to Students" on pages 16, 17, and 28.

   Once students are comfortable with these "mini" performances, teachers must create opportunities for students to play in public, so that they will get used to the idea of getting up on stage and playing for others. Studio group lessons or performance classes are perfect for trial performances, then take it to the next step and invite family or friends to a performance class.

   Try these different performance venues and you will be pleased with the results. The "tiered" approach helps performance to become a natural part of piano study.

2. Make sure that your students have the opportunity to perform pieces well within their technical range. These performances will help build student confidence and will make a huge difference when they are playing more challenging repertoire.

3. Have students practice concentrating on the tempo, mood, and dynamics of the piece before beginning to play.

FF1459

4. Coach students on how to walk purposefully *to* the piano, adjust the bench, and check their position relative to the piano. Have them practice this a lot in the lesson and at home. Familiarity with the process really helps.

5. Talk to your students about how to finish the piece. Coach them to stay with the music until the piece is over. Discuss how they will move at the end of the piece: i.e., quickly moving the hands away from the keyboard, or slowly lifting the hands with the lifting of the pedal, depending on the repertoire.

6. Coach students how to bow and walk purposefully *away* from the piano. Again, practice this together often so that it feels natural to them.

7. Remind students to keep the recital in perspective. The recital piece should be one of several the student is working on, so that they understand that there is "life after the recital."

8. If possible, have a practice session in the performance location. Encourage your students to focus on what they can control and remind them that although a piano may feel differently, their technique will not "go away."

9. Have your students listen to the companion CD. Not only does this give them ideas on how to interpret the pieces, it builds an intuitive knowledge of how the pieces sound, which helps increase confidence and comfort.

The goal is to instill in our students the excitement of playing for others and to demystify the process. There is nothing quite like communicating a piece of music to an audience and then enjoying their positive reaction to it. With our help, our students can perform up to their potential in public and enjoy this exciting and rewarding experience.

ORGANIZATION OF THE SERIES
IN RECITAL • THROUGHOUT THE YEAR

The series is carefully leveled into the following six categories: Early Elementary, Elementary, Late Elementary, Early Intermediate, Intermediate, and Late Intermediate. Each of the works has been selected for its artistic as well as its pedagogical merit.

Book One — Early Elementary, reinforces the following concepts:

- Basic notes, such as quarter, half, dotted half, and whole notes, are used.

- Only $\frac{3}{4}$ and $\frac{4}{4}$ time signatures are used.

- Students experience movement up and down the keyboard, with 8va signs.

- Students sometimes use the pedal to create a big sound.

- Students play with a detached as well as a smooth touch.

- Most of the pieces call for only limited use of hands-together playing.

- Pieces reinforce basic musical terminology and symbols such as *forte*, *piano*, and repeat signs.

- Pieces use middle C and G position as well as other basic hand positions.

- Basic keys — C major, G major, F major, A minor (written using accidentals instead of key signatures) are used.

All of the pieces in Book One may be played as solos. *The Two-Headed Monster* was composed as an equal part duet. Many of the solos have teacher duet parts to enhance the overall sound of the piece.

TABLE OF CONTENTS

Distant Bells

Elizabeth W. Greenleaf

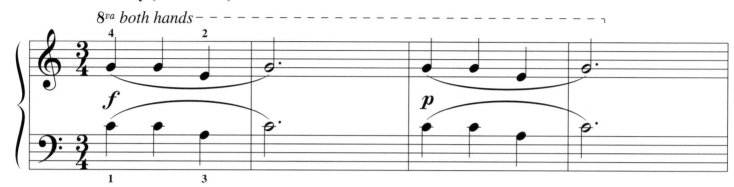

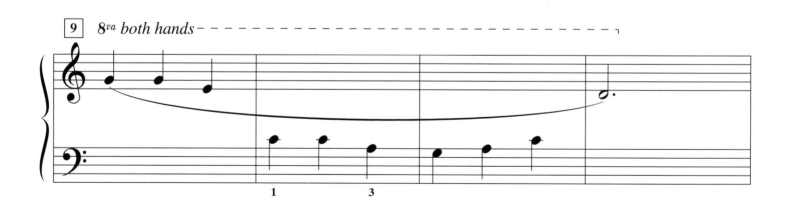

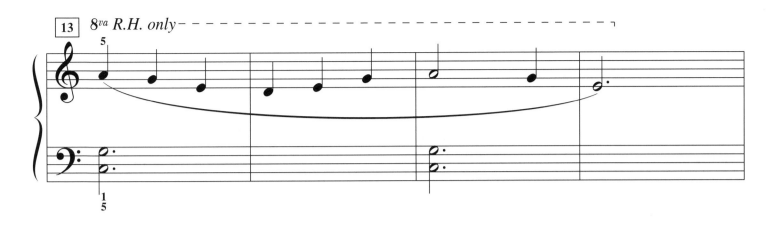

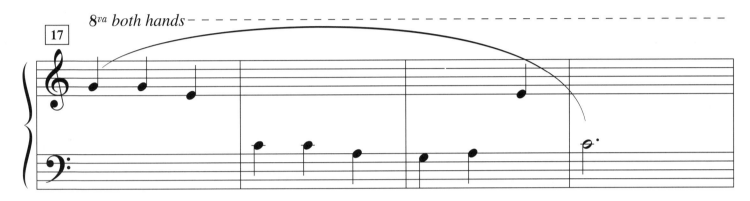

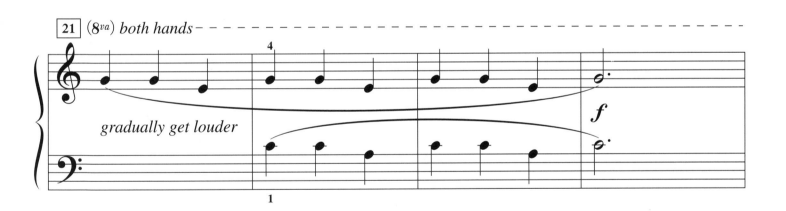

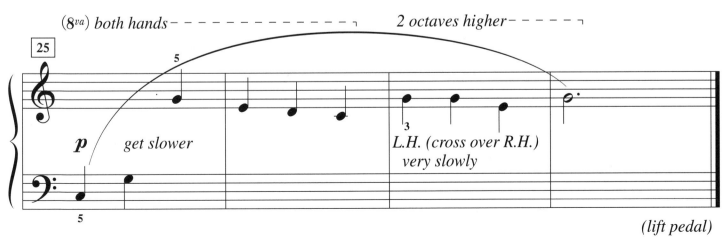

FIVE O'CLOCK ROCK

Christopher Goldston

With energy! (♩ = 152 or faster)

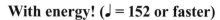

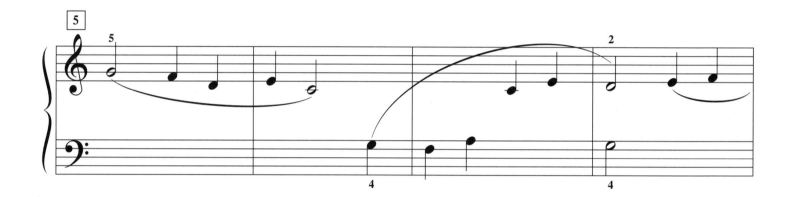

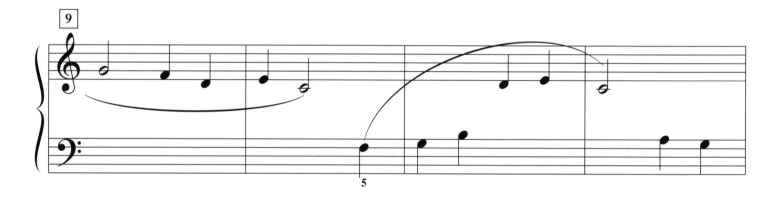

The Two-Headed Monster
Secondo

Kevin R. Olson

In a bad mood (♩ = 120-144)
Play both hands one octave lower throughout and make the quarter notes short!

THE TWO-HEADED MONSTER
Primo

Kevin R. Olson

In a bad mood (♩ = 120-144)
Play both hands one octave higher throughout and make the quarter notes short!

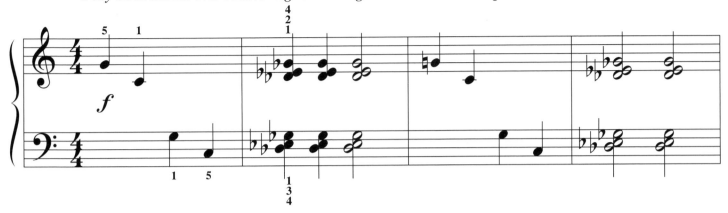

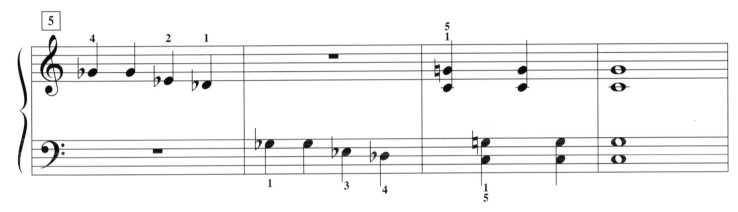

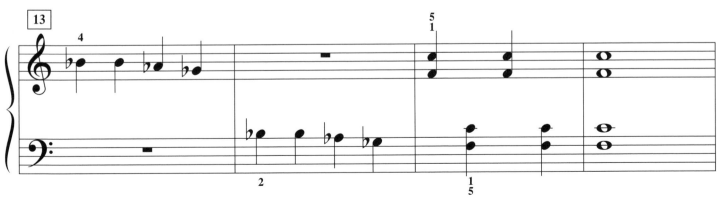

FF1459

Secondo

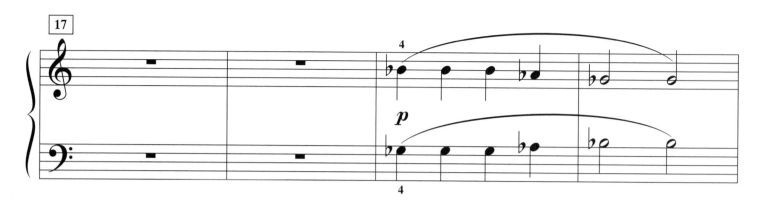

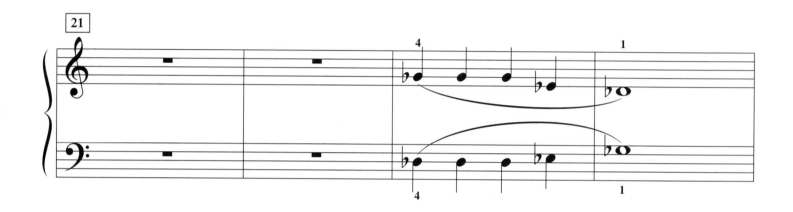

Play the lowest C on the piano!

Primo

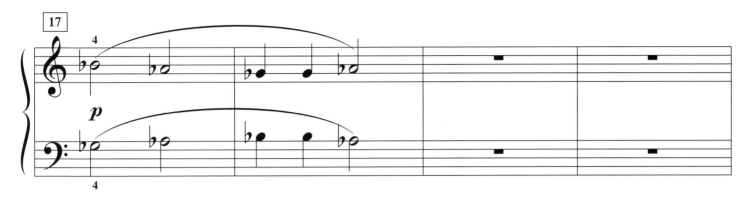

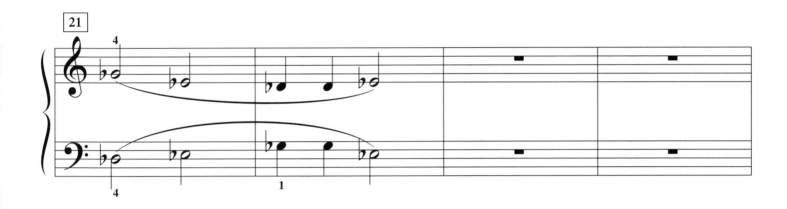

Play the highest C on the piano!

Theme from The Moldau

Bedřich Smetana
arr. Timothy Brown

Teacher Accompaniment: (*Student plays one octave higher*)

A NOTE TO STUDENTS

Welcome to the wonderful world of performing. Performing in public is a special skill that can be learned, just like learning how to ride a bike! It might seem a bit scary at first, but once you learn this skill, performing can be a whole lot of fun!

Here are two keys to successful and enjoyable performances:

- Prepare well beforehand

- Practice performing in front of others

Preparation:
Here is a list of things to do to make sure you know your piece extremely well: (Place a check in the box for each day you complete the task and start four weeks before the recital.)

Can you play the entire piece, hands alone? (Listening to each individual part helps you to be completely aware of what each hand is playing.)

Can you sing or hum the melody away from the piano?

Can you start your piece at four different places in the music? (You and your teacher can mark with a star ☆ four good starting places).

Can you play the piece from beginning to end at "half tempo"? ("Half tempo" means to play it with all of the correct rhythms, notes, and dynamics, but at half of the speed you would play it when performing it.)

After playing the piece, ask yourself: Did it sound like the title suggests? Did I bring the piece to life?

Listen to the recording of your recital piece for ideas on how to play it. You can mark directly in your score what you hear.

Starting four weeks before your actual performance, practice these strategies every day. It might be difficult to do all of these at first, but the more you practice, the easier they will become. Remember, if you prepare well, the performance day will be easy and fun!

> You can use this page as a practice guide for every recital piece you play in this book!

PERFORMING FOR AN AUDIENCE

When you have worked hard to learn your recital piece(s), then you are ready to play for others. This is part of the fun of learning how to play the piano — to share the music!

The following is a list of performance options. Check them off as you complete them. You can play for each of these groups many times!! Once you do this, you will be confident that you are ready to perform this piece in a recital:

☐ First, play at home for your stuffed animals or family pet

☐ Then, play for a special friend

☐ Play at home for your family

☐ Your teacher might have group classes – this is an excellent way to try playing in front of others!

☐ Other venue: (a music class at school, or for a church function.)

_____

You can use this page as a practice guide for every recital piece you play in this book!

To learn the **Steps for a Winning Performance**, turn to page 28.

ODE TO JOY

Theme from *Symphony No. 9*

Ludwig van Beethoven
arr. Edwin McLean

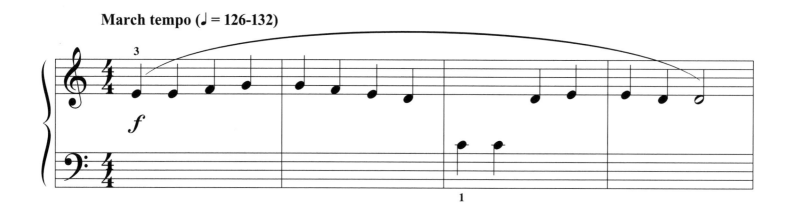

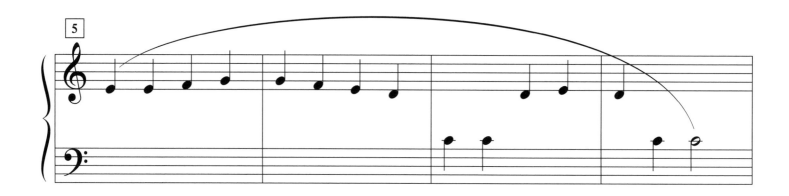

Teacher Accompaniment: (*Student plays one octave higher*)

Morning
from Peer Gynt Suite No. 1
Op. 46

Edvard Grieg
arr. Edwin McLean

Flowing (♩ = 144-152)

Teacher Accompaniment: (*Student plays as written*)

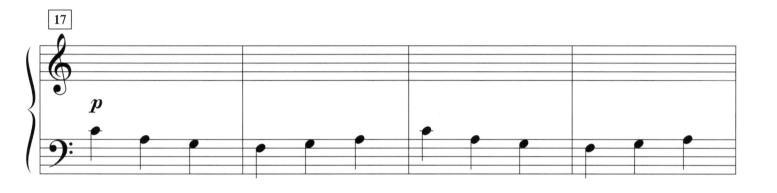

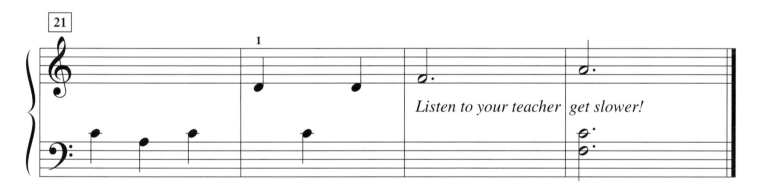

Listen to your teacher get slower!

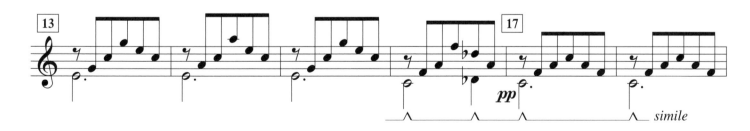

simile

(L.H. over R.H.)

rit.

Hear the Wind Blowing!

Mary Leaf

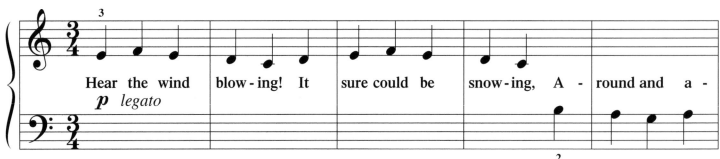

Hear the wind blow-ing! It sure could be snow-ing, A - round and a-

p legato

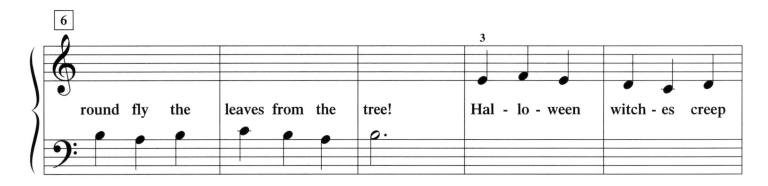

round fly the leaves from the tree! Hal - lo - ween witch - es creep

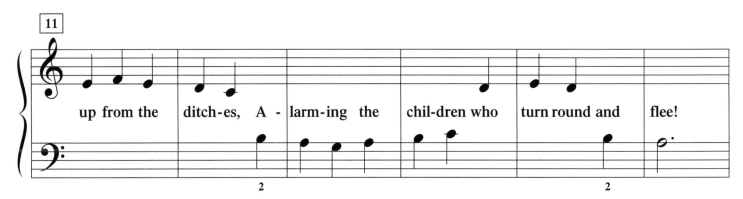

up from the ditch-es, A - larm-ing the chil-dren who turn round and flee!

Teacher Accompaniment: (*Student plays one octave higher*)

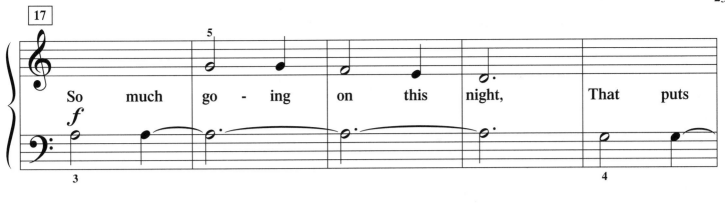

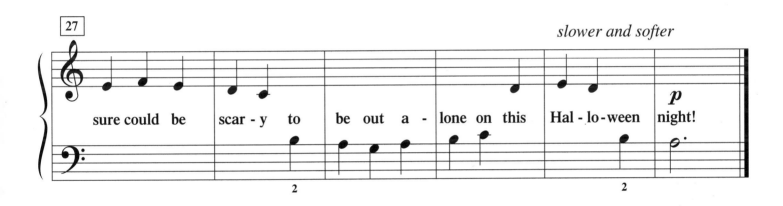

Away in a Manger

Traditional
arr. Melody Bober

Peacefully (♩ = 96)

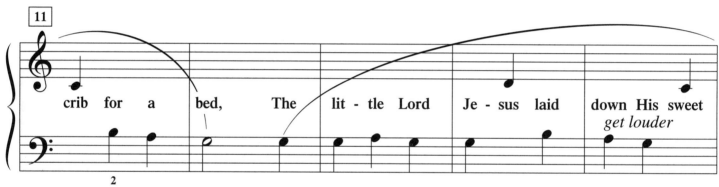

Teacher Accompaniment: (*Student plays one octave higher*)

When Johnny Comes Marching Home Again

Traditional
arr. Kevin R. Olson

Teacher Accompaniment: (*Student plays one octave higher*)

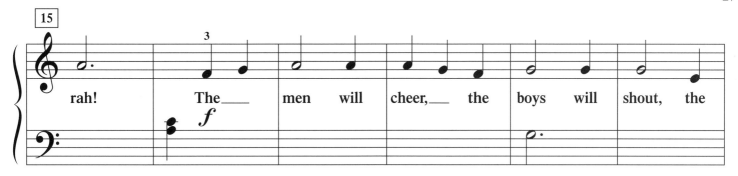

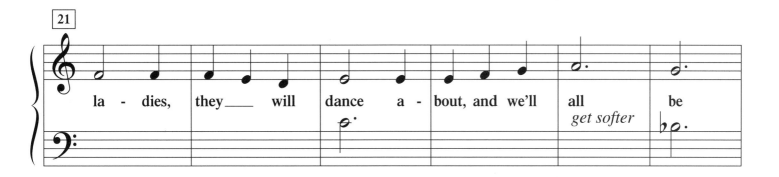

STEPS FOR A WINNING PERFORMANCE

- Practice walking to the piano with confidence and with purpose.

- Practice standing in front of the piano bench, nodding your head, and smiling at the audience.

- Practice sitting at the bench and making sure you are seated at the proper height as well as distance from the keyboard.

- Practice breathing before you begin, and think about the speed, mood, and dynamics of the piece before beginning to play.

- Practice staying with the music while you play! This means that you think about the notes, dynamics, and phrasing as you play, and listen to yourself every single moment.

- Practice placing your hands in your lap after you finish playing. Remember to bow. It is a way to say, "thank you" to your audience for listening.

ABOUT THE COMPOSERS/ARRANGERS

Melody Bober

Piano instructor, music teacher, composer, clinician—Melody Bober has been active in music education for over 25 years. As a composer, her goal is to create exciting and challenging pieces that are strong teaching tools to promote a lifelong love, understanding, and appreciation for music. Pedagogy, ear training, and musical expression are fundamentals of Melody's teaching, as well as fostering composition skills in her students.

Melody graduated with highest honors from the University of Illinois with a degree in music education, and later received a master's degree in piano performance. She maintains a large private studio, performs in numerous regional events, and conducts workshops across the country. She and her husband Jeff reside in Minnesota.

Timothy Brown

Composition has always been a natural form of self-expression for Timothy Brown. His Montessori-influenced philosophy has greatly helped define his approach as a teacher and composer of educational music. His composition originates from a love of improvisation at the piano and his personal goal of writing music that will help release the student's imagination.

Mr. Brown holds two degrees in piano performance, including a master's degree from the University of North Texas. His many honors include a "Commissioned for Clavier" magazine article, and first prize award in the Fifth Aliénor International Harpsichord Competition for his solo composition *Suite Española*. As a clinician, Mr. Brown has presented numerous clinics and most recently represented FJH Music with his presentation at the 2000 World Piano Pedagogy Conference. Currently living in Dallas, Mr. Brown teaches piano and composition at the Harry Stone Montessori Magnet School. He frequently serves as an adjudicator for piano and composition contests, and performs with his wife as duo-pianists.

Christopher Goldston

Christopher Goldston holds a Master of Music degree in piano performance and pedagogy from Northwestern University, and a Bachelor of Music degree in piano performance from the University of North Carolina–Greensboro. He lives in Chicago, Illinois, and has taught at Sherwood Conservatory of Music and Harper College.

In 1991, Mr. Goldston received the National Federation of Music Clubs Lynn Freeman Olson Composition Award for his first composition, *Night Train*. Since then, he has written numerous pieces for piano, voice, and chamber ensemble, including *Thesis for Wind Quintet*, which won the 1993 North Carolina State Music Teachers Association Collegiate Composition Contest.

Mr. Goldston has taught piano for over ten years and enjoys composing and arranging pieces for his students. Many of them have created pieces of their own under his guidance and have received top prizes in state competitions. Mr. Goldston has also served as chair of the composition contest for Illinois State Music Teachers Association and MTNA East Central Division.

Elizabeth W. Greenleaf

Elizabeth W. Greenleaf received a Piano Teaching Certificate and a Bachelor of Music degree in composition from Florida State University, and a Master of Music degree in piano performance from Louisiana State University.

Elizabeth has been active as a composer, performer, and teacher for over twenty-five years. She has performed many recitals, both as an accompanist for instrumentalists and singers, and as a chamber music player. Her students have ranged from preschoolers to senior citizens, and she has taught at all levels from beginning to advanced. Recently retired from teaching, Elizabeth enjoys composing to meet the needs of students. Her music has received high praise from top teachers throughout the country.

Mary Leaf

Mary Leaf is an independent piano teacher specializing in early elementary through intermediate level students. She enjoys writing music that is descriptive, expressive, imaginative, and fun, while still being musically sound.

Mary received a music education degree from the University of Washington and has done continuing education in pedagogy at North Dakota State University. She has composed and arranged music for a family recorder ensemble, and has been active as a performer, accompanist, handbell ringer, and choir member at her church. She is also active in area contests as an accompanist. Mary and her husband Ron have five children and live in Bismarck, North Dakota.

Edwin McLean

Edwin McLean is a composer living in Coconut Grove, Florida. He is a graduate of the Yale School of Music, where he studied with Krzysztof Penderecki and Jacob Druckman. He also holds degrees in music theory and piano performance from the University of Colorado. The recipient of several grants and awards, including The MacDowell Colony, the John Work Award, the Woods Chandler Prize (Yale), Meet the Composer, Florida Arts Council, and others, he has also won the Aliénor Composition Competition for his work *Sonata for Harpsichord*, published by The FJH Music Company Inc. and recorded by Elaine Funaro (Into the Millennium, Gasparo GSCD-331).

Since 1979, Edwin McLean has arranged the music of some of today's best known recording artists. Currently, he is senior editor as well as MIDI orchestrator for FJH Music.

Kevin Olson

Kevin Olson is an active pianist, composer, and faculty member at Elmhurst College near Chicago, Illinois, where he teaches classical and jazz piano, music theory, and electronic music. He holds a Doctor of Education degree from National-Louis University, and bachelor's and master's degrees in music composition and theory from Brigham Young University. Before teaching at Elmhurst College, he held a visiting professor position at Humboldt State University in California. A native of Utah, Kevin began composing at the age of five. When he was twelve, his composition *An American Trainride* received the Overall First Prize at the 1983 National PTA Convention in Albuquerque, New Mexico. Since then, he has been a composer-in-residence at the National Conference on Piano Pedagogy and has written music for the American Piano Quartet, Chicago a cappella, the Rich Matteson Jazz Festival, among others. Kevin maintains a large piano studio, teaching students of a variety of ages and abilities. Many of the needs of his own piano students have inspired his nearly forty books and solos published by The FJH Music Company Inc., which he joined as a writer in 1994.